COME *and* BEHOLD HIM

A CHRISTMAS DEVOTIONAL

BroadStreet
PUBLISHING

BroadStreet Publishing Group, LLC.
Savage, Minnesota, USA
Broadstreetpublishing.com

COME AND BEHOLD HIM

978-1-4245-6002-8
978-1-4245-6033-2 (ebook)

Devotional entries composed by Michelle Cox and Julie Lavender.

Design by Chris Garborg | garborgdesign.com
Editorial services by Michelle Winger | literallyprecise.com

Printed in China.
19 20 21 22 23 24 25   7 6 5 4 3 2 1

The Lord himself will give you a sign.
Behold, the virgin shall conceive and bear a son,
and shall call his name Immanuel.

ISAIAH 7:14 ESV

Contents

Introduction

Christmas is often called the most wonderful time of the year—and with good reason. Our homes become festive and cozy. Children are so full of excitement it's a wonder they don't pop. Families spend time together, making memories to last a lifetime. Community buildings and churches feature gorgeous decorations. Sets are painted for Christmas plays, and choirs practice beautiful music that fills the air with joy.

Love-filled gifts are wrapped and placed under our trees. Christmas lights bathe everything in a soft glow. Villages with tiny figurines line our mantles and tables, and trees laden with ornaments, lights, and garland make us smile.

And, oh my, the delightful foods that we enjoy at Christmas! Everyone makes their specialties, often gathering the entire family to bake lopsided sugar cookies or a favorite family recipe.

The dining table looks like a page from a magazine, piled high with platters of meat, countless sides, and so many desserts it looks like we could feed everyone in the neighborhood.

Is there anything more special than the holiday season? After all, it's a birthday party for Jesus. Nothing could possibly be more important than celebrating the birth of that baby in the manger, and Christmas gives us the chance to worship him.

Let each day of this devotional draw you in as you come to behold the wonder of Jesus and celebrate the one who changed the world forever.

COME
AND
BEHOLD
HIM...

Immanuel

Humble Surroundings

"Today in the town of David
a Savior has been born to you;
he is the Messiah, the Lord.
This will be a sign to you:
You will find a baby wrapped in cloths
and lying in a manger."

LUKE 2:11-12 NIV

COME AND BEHOLD A SAVIOR

WHO IS ACCESSIBLE TO ALL.

The Biltmore Estate in Asheville, North Carolina, is the largest privately-owned home in the United States. Guests can purchase tickets to tour the ornate castle-like house that is filled with priceless historical treasures and enjoy the grounds with their breathtaking views of the mountains, intricately designed gardens, and quaint stables.

Without any doubt, the best time to visit the Biltmore Estate is at Christmas. Candle-lit luminaries line the massive driveway, guiding the way into the one-of-a-kind home. The banquet hall features a live 35-foot tree that takes about fifty men to carry in, and that tree only goes halfway toward the top of the seventy-foot ceiling. Hundreds of poinsettias flood the house, and in the days leading to Christmas, choirs and stringed quartets fill the hallways with lovely Christmas carols.

Flickering candles add to the ambiance, and there's even a whole pig roasting on the spit in the kitchen fireplace. It smells really good in there. It's impossible to leave the estate without being in the Christmas spirit.

This massive home—built many years ago by a rich and famous family—is an impressive place to visit, but most of us would never feel at home there because we don't feel like we fit into that world of expensive luxury. And that should make us think about something: God could have sent his Son to earth in any manner he chose. It would have been fitting for the Savior of the universe to be born into one of these luxurious homes.

But that's not how God did it because he knew that many of us would never be comfortable in those circumstances. Instead, God sent Jesus to us in humble surroundings, in the lowly place where the animals slept, so all of us would feel at ease to come close to him.

What a special gift this Christmas to know that the Savior who created the world is accessible to each of us. He's available to be our comforter, our provider, our guide, and our friend.

Jesus, thank you for humbling yourself so you're approachable for all of us. I'm grateful that the welcome mat is always out at the foot of the cross, and that those who come to you will always be greeted with love and grace.

A CHRISTMAS GIFT

Purchase an unbreakable manger set so children can be hands-on with it. Consider cutting small lengths of hay that the children can add to the manger when they do something nice—to help cushion it for the baby Jesus. On Christmas Eve, let the children (and maybe even some of the big kids) put the figures into place as your family reads the Christmas story together.

A Moment to Ponder

Take a few moments to think about a Savior who is big enough to create the world, yet willing to humble himself for us.

A Sweet Recipe

That you and I may be mutually encouraged by each other's faith.

ROMANS 1:12 NIV

BE GRATEFUL FOR OPPORTUNITIES
TO COME AND BEHOLD JESUS AS YOU
FELLOWSHIP TOGETHER AT CHRISTMAS.

I love to host Christmas parties for family and friends. Several years ago, I came up with an idea that led to a fun, easy, and amazingly delicious Christmas get-together. I invited about fifteen of my girlfriends to come to my house one morning during the holidays and asked them to bring a sweet item and a savory dish that they wanted to try from posts on Pinterest or Facebook. Since most of us are good at saving these recipes but never actually making them, this would give us the opportunity to try more than thirty new recipes.

I instructed the attendees to do the prep work at home and then we all gathered in my kitchen to finish preparing the recipes together. It was so much fun! We laughed while we cooked. There were cheesy potatoes and a chicken casserole. There were spiced pecans and appetizers, all beautifully decorated for Christmas. There were Christmas-tree-topped cupcakes with the best buttercream frosting we'd ever had. And the list went on and on.

Once the recipes were completed and everything had been arranged on the kitchen island, we were all blown away with how beautiful everything looked. It was a feast for the eyes. Once we started sampling all the newly-prepared foods, we realized it was also a feast for the taste buds.

We discovered some definite keepers and a few recipes that didn't look anything like what they had in the pictures. The food was terrific, but what made the day so special was the sweet fellowship that we all had as we celebrated the reason for the season. We talked about our families, Christmas, and precious moments we'd had with God.

We shared about God's faithfulness, about the blessings he's given us, and about the gift of our friendship. That time together was so awesome, and we were grateful for the opportunity to come and behold him as we fellowshipped together at Christmas.

Delightful treats. Special friends. A sweet time together as we celebrated Christmas and who it is all about. It truly doesn't get much better than that.

Lord, I thank you for the gift of family and friends. I'm especially grateful for friends who also love you, and for the sweet fellowship we have as we celebrate you at Christmas.

A CHRISTMAS GIFT

Consider hosting a Christmas party for people who are sometimes left out of those celebrations. Invite a group of single parents, senior citizens, or those who have just moved into the community. You don't have to do anything fancy or elaborate. A warm welcome will be a special gift to them (and one that will please the heart of God) this Christmas.

A Moment to Ponder

Why is Christmas such a special time to fellowship with friends who also love God?

A Holy Night

Let everything that has breath praise the LORD.
Praise the LORD!

PSALM 150:6 NASB

COME AND BEHOLD HIM IN WORSHIP
AND THANK HIM FOR A HOLY NIGHT
THAT CHANGED THE WORLD FOREVER.

$\mathcal{D}$ays are always busy at our house, but at Christmas, it seems like the action sometimes ramps up to a crazy level. Some days I feel as if I'm on a merry-go-round that keeps going faster and faster, and I can't get off.

The to-do list stretches from North Carolina to Kansas. The days are filled with fighting the crowds at the mall and sometimes searching for that one illusive must-have gift. Piles of presents are stacked high until we can find time to wrap them. Stacks of Christmas cards sit waiting to be signed and addressed. A variety of cookies must be baked to deliver to neighbors, business associates, and the staff at church. And the house must be turned into a Christmas wonderland.

There are Christmas programs to attend at schools and cupcakes to bake for class parties. Mom's Taxi Service ferries children to Christmas play practices and other activities. All of this is on top of the normal mountains of laundry, meal prep, homework assistance, straightening the house, and conquering the endless stream of dirty dishes.

Is it any wonder that Jesus sometimes gets pushed to the side in the middle of his own celebration?

One of my favorite times during the Christmas season comes late each evening after my family has gone to bed. I love to head into our family room and turn on all the Christmas lights. I sit there and soak in the warm coziness of the scene. The ornaments reflect our family memories. The Bethlehem village makes me think about what it was like in the days when Jesus was born. The Nativity set reminds me of my children and grandchildren who have played with it as they learned the greatest story ever told. The Christmas tree symbolizes a tree made into a cross that hung on Calvary.

It's a time when I can come and behold him in worship and thank him for a holy night that changed the world forever.

Father, remind me to make time to worship you during the holidays: to celebrate the holy night when the angels sang to celebrate your arrival. Help me to never lose the wonder of a babe in a manger who came to save the world.

A CHRISTMAS GIFT

Gather around the tree together during the Christmas season and talk about why Jesus is worthy of our praise. Have each person write down some of the blessings they've received that year and place those slips of paper in a basket. Make time to read them all together on Christmas Day.

A Moment to Ponder

Think about Jesus and how different your life would be if he hadn't come. (But the good news is that he did.) Then thank him for all the ways he has impacted you and your family.

Good News

The angel said to them, "Fear not, for behold, I bring you good news of great joy that will be for all the people."

LUKE 2:10 ESV

WHEN WE REMEMBER THAT GOD WANTS
ALL TO COME AND BEHOLD JESUS,
IT MAKES US WANT TO SHARE
THE GOOD NEWS WITH EVERYONE.

*M*y sister's church hosts an event called "Journey to Bethlehem" every other year at Christmas. It's a huge production that takes a large number of animals and hundreds of actors and actresses who transform into Roman soldiers, shepherds and angels, Elizabeth and Zacharias, Mary and Joseph, and Bethlehem townspeople.

Tree roots and the uneven ground that's washed in darkness make the journey from stage to stage difficult, and I cling to my husband for balance. I avoid eye contact with the Roman centurions who take their roles so seriously that my heart pounds in fear. A boat ride takes us toward the crowded streets of Bethlehem, where we sample grapes and cheese and bits of bread. The fire in the center of town warms my hands before we're shuffled into the next scene, the one with Mary and Joseph and baby Jesus.

A spotlight shines heavenward and an angel shouts to the shepherds, "I bring you good tidings of great joy which will be to all people."

My church hosts an event with the same name at Christmas, too, in a church member's field. Though smaller, the message is the same, with the aroma of bread, fire, farm animals, spices and perfume, and dust and mud. I recognize the faces of almost everyone I pass, not only the costumed ones, but the community visitors from other churches too. They're folks I've known almost my whole life. But each time I attend the one in my sister's larger town an hour away, a stark contrast exists.

Yet the angel's good news applied to everyone, to the throngs of unfamiliar faces surrounding me. I'm glad God sent Jesus for me, but I have to remember that no one is excluded. *All* means *all*. I can't pick and choose who gets to hear the message. When I remember that God wants all to come and behold Jesus, it makes me want to share the good news with everyone, not just those who look a lot like me.

Dear God, help me remember that the night Jesus was born, Mary and Joseph were surrounded by a sea of unfamiliar faces in Bethlehem, some that may have looked a lot like them, but many that might not have. Remind me often that your plan is for everyone to come to a saving knowledge of Jesus Christ, and that when you say all, you mean all. Help me to share the good news with everyone I meet.

A CHRISTMAS GIFT

Is there an area of need in your community where you've never served—perhaps where the recipients look very different from you physically, economically, or spiritually? Reach out to those individuals and share the good news that the angel spoke of, and then find out how you can serve them this Christmas.

A Moment to Ponder

Can you think of a time when you were excluded, maybe as a child on the playground or later in life as an adult? How did that make you feel? Why should you not want to exclude anyone from hearing the good news of Jesus' birth?

A Long Way to Go

Joseph also went up from Galilee, out of the city of
Nazareth, into Judea, to the city of David, which is called
Bethlehem, because he was of the house and lineage of
David, to be registered with Mary, his betrothed wife,
who was with child.

LUKE 2:4-5 NKJV

YOU CAN COME AND BEHOLD HIM
WHEN YOU LEAN INTO HIM FOR
GUIDANCE ON HOW TO ACCOMPLISH
THE TASKS AT HAND.

I try to imagine the difficult journey that Joseph and Mary took to Bethlehem. I can barely fathom how the couple traveled that far, probably on a donkey, with Mary huge with child. How did they manage their food and clothing? Where did they sleep along the way? And goodness, gracious, how in the world could Mary get comfortable enough to sleep *anywhere* in that condition, especially after riding a donkey all day?

It reminds me of a challenging journey my family took one year near Christmas. When a sudden snowstorm blanketed our original itinerary from Washington State to Jacksonville, Florida, my husband and I pointed our two vehicles south and kept trudging on because another storm was right behind the first one.

It was terrifying. For the entire state of Utah, the tire tracks ahead of us were the only piece of landscape that wasn't completely blanketed in snow. And the worst was when the windshield wipers froze mid-wipe and needed thawing underneath a bridge. We prayed mightily, mile after mile.

Mary and Joseph had a much more difficult journey than we did, and with God's help, they pressed on and moved forward. They trusted God to guide them along the way and never gave up. For God to have chosen them to be the parents of his Son, Jesus, it indicated a track record that they'd spent their whole lives allowing God to guide them.

When I get bogged down with my lengthy to-do list at Christmas, I think about Mary and Joseph pushing forward in their journey. I take a deep breath and ask God to guide me each step of the way until I get to the final destination, whether that's the end of my shopping list, or the batch of goodies baked for the family dinner, or the last Christmas card sealed and mailed. I've learned that I can come and behold him when I lean into him for guidance to accomplish my tasks at hand. I'm positive that's what Mary and Joseph did.

God, thank you for guiding my path day after day, mile after mile. Help me to lean into you and to trust you to show me the way. When I get bogged down with too much busyness, show me what's really important and what you'd have me do.

A CHRISTMAS GIFT

With family input, make a list of tasks that need to get done over the holidays. Place the list in a location where other family members can see it. Ask family members to pray over these tasks each time they see the list. For example, let the notation to "shop for extended family members" be a reminder to pray for each person by name. Or, let "take soup to a sick neighbor" be a reminder to pray for those who are sick or whose cupboards are bare this Christmas. Pray for each notation in similar fashion.

A Moment to Ponder

Think about a time that you depended on God to guide you through a difficult journey or situation, like Mary and Joseph did. Make sure to share that memory with your family. Share specifically how you prayed and how God was faithful to guide you each step of the way.

COME
AND
BEHOLD
HIM...

the Messiah

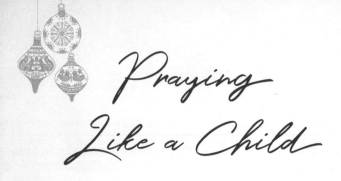

Praying Like a Child

Pray without ceasing.
1 Thessalonians 5:17 nasb

Come and behold him through your
prayers even when it seems like
answers take a long time.

One of my family's favorite Christmas traditions for years has been taking part in Samaritan's Purse "Operation Christmas Child" shoebox ministry. We love picking out small dolls, toy cars, bouncy balls, crayons, books, toiletry items, hard candy, and stuffed animals to fill the boxes.

One year was extra special. Each of the four children packed a box. As soon as the packages left our care, my eight-year-old daughter began to pray for her recipient. Every night, she ended her prayers with these words: "Please help my box to get there safely. Please help the little girl who will get my box and bless her family."

My daughter prayed. And prayed. And prayed. For more than a year and a half, almost every night.

In exasperation one night, her older brother finally told her, "I think your box has made it there. You can stop praying now." But my eleven-year-old son didn't understand the love that God had given his sister for a little girl she'd never met.

Less than a week later, we received a torn letter on blue stationery in the mail. The only word we recognized amongst the foreign symbols was *India*. But we could see the beautiful face of a precious little girl in a photograph.

I remembered that a church friend grew up in India. His face beamed when he opened the envelope. "Guess what? I can read this!" He read the letter word for word.

It was worth the wait. And the prayers. And you better believe we all prayed fervently for every Christmas box we packed from then on. Christmas became even sweeter each year because of a shoebox.

Our family learned that day to come and behold him through our prayers, even when it seems like answers take a long time. Prayer is an act of obedience. It allows us to praise and worship God through our words and to make requests. Talking to God regularly and consistently grows our relationship with the heavenly Father and strengthens our faith. I'm so glad God hears our prayers even when they're for a Christmas shoebox filled with candy and toys.

God, I'm thankful that you love me so much that you want to have a relationship with me, and you sent a baby in a manager to make that possible. Thank you for the gift of communicating with you through prayer. Thank you for hearing and answering my prayers even when those answers take what seems to be a long time or when those answers aren't exactly what I planned.

A CHRISTMAS GIFT

Consider adopting a family or some children who might need extra help over the holidays. Make homemade gifts and goodies. Write notes about why Christmas is special to your family and what it means to you that God sent his only Son as a newborn baby—that he'd grow up to be the Savior of the world through his death on the cross. Deliver the goodies personally or coordinate through an agency in your hometown that serves those in need over the holidays.

A Moment to Ponder

Have you ever experienced a Christmas miracle? Maybe a fervent prayer was answered or maybe you received healing over Christmas. Perhaps a reconciliation took place during the holidays. What might you do this Christmas to help be the answer to someone's prayers?

Gifts from the Heart

When they had come into the house,
they saw the young Child with Mary His mother,
and fell down and worshiped Him. And when they had
opened their treasures, they presented gifts to Him:
gold, frankincense, and myrrh.

MATTHEW 2:11 NKJV

WHEN WE COME AND BEHOLD THE KING IN
ALL HIS GLORY, IT MAKES US WANT TO GIVE
HIM OUR VERY BEST GIFTS AND TREASURES.

---

*M*y dad passed away in September of that year, and my eleven-year-old daughter wanted to give her grieving Mema something extra special for Christmas. "I'll crochet her a granny square blanket," she said excitedly. "A blue one, because blue is her favorite color."

A couple of years back, my mom and I had taught my daughter to crochet. And, when I was a little girl, my mom and both grandmas taught me the stitches. As the fourth generation to learn the craft of crocheting, she began working weeks before Christmas to create her gift of love.

"I'll treasure this always!" Mema exclaimed on Christmas morning. "This took a long time to make and you made it just for me. How special." I'm not sure if the tears fell because Mema appreciated the handmade gift or if it stirred memories of my sick daddy wrapped up in the blanket his mom had crocheted so long ago. I suspect both.

My daughter's gift reminded me of the wisemen's gifts to Jesus—they gave their very best treasures to the baby King. Nothing but the best would do for the Savior of the world. And they gave much of their time in travel to deliver those gifts in person.

I couldn't help but ask myself, *Do I give my very best gifts to Jesus?* I don't have gold and frankincense and myrrh, but do I give my tithes and offerings cheerfully and timely? Do I read his word with attention to detail or am I easily distracted? Do I use the talents he gave me to serve him in my church and in the community? Do I use my writing to share the gospel and point people toward him? Do I train up my children in the Word? Do I honor and respect my husband and use kind words in my home?

There are lots of ways I can give gifts to Jesus: physically, emotionally, and spiritually. When I come and behold the King in all his glory, it makes me want to give him my very best gifts and treasures.

Dear Jesus, I know there is nothing I can do or give you that can make you love me more than you already do. Because you are the King of the world, it makes me want to give you my very best treasures.

A CHRISTMAS GIFT

Make edible wisemen with your family using a sugar cone turned upside down for the body and a large marshmallow for the head. Press the marshmallow into the pointed end of the cone to make it stay in place. Wrap pressed fruit pieces around the cone for royal robes. Then talk about gifts that you can give baby Jesus. Perhaps you'll list physical gifts like volunteer work in the community or a monetary donation to someone in need. Perhaps you'll list things like "doing my best in school" or "sharing Jesus to a coworker." Or maybe you'll plan to read through the entire Bible by this time next year. What gifts can you give Jesus?

A Moment to Ponder

Why do you think it was so important for the wisemen to see baby Jesus in person? What can you do to draw nearer to Jesus?

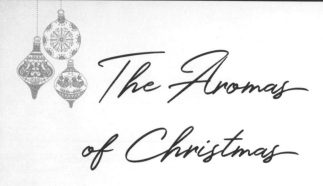

The Aromas of Christmas

*Walk in love, as Christ also has loved us
and given Himself for us,
an offering and a sacrifice to God
for a sweet-smelling aroma.*

EPHESIANS 5:2 NKJV

TEACH CHILDREN TO COME AND BEHOLD

JESUS, SO THEY'LL SHARE

THE SWEET AROMA OF HIS LOVE

WITH THE NEXT GENERATION.

There's something special about the aromas of Christmas. My dad always said, "Now it smells like Christmas!" as I sautéed the celery and onion for the dressing. At my aunt's house, those aromas were always from the delicious treats she made each holiday season. One year, she tried all the recipes from her new magazine, and if someone could have bottled that fragrance, they'd have made a fortune.

My aunt is one of the reasons I love to bake. And just as she taught me so many years before, I love to make Christmas goodies with my grandchildren: a tradition started when their daddies were small. The little ones are so precious as they stir the dough or as they add ingredients.

Our sugar cookies are sometimes lopsided. My young bakers are often covered in flour, with sticky faces from where they've licked the beaters. The kitchen looks like a hurricane has been through it. But laughing together as we bake, seeing their joy in the moments, and making precious Christmas memories is worth every minute of clean-up. And the bonus is seeing their expressions as they sample what we've made.

I hope they'll always remember these times. In years to

come, I hope the aroma of cookies will take them back to wonderful Christmas memories in Grandmama's kitchen. But even more than that, I hope that the memories we make each Christmas as we read the Christmas story, pray together on Christmas Eve thanking God for his many blessings, and attend church and Christmas plays together will also provide a sweet aroma of God's love—a fragrance that will keep them close to him for the rest of their lives.

Someday my precious little ones will have their own children. I hope they'll carry on the cookie baking tradition, but even more, my heart's desire is that they'll teach their children to come and behold him, and that they'll share the sweet aroma of God's love with the next generation.

Lord, thank you for the sweet aroma and the daily reminders of your love. Just as the aromas of baking can bring back memories of long ago, help the moments that we've shared worshipping you and serving you at Christmas, and throughout the year, remind my family of your precious love.

A CHRISTMAS GIFT

Christmas is a wonderful time to share God's love especially with people who are hungry for someone to care about them. Bake cookies or loaf-sized cakes with your family (or purchase some). Package them in clear baking wrap and tie a pretty ribbon around them. Then add a note that says, "Jesus is the reason for the season—and he loves you!" Pass them out to homeless people in your town or drop your baked goods off at a homeless shelter. I can promise that the sweet aromas of your cookies and cakes, and the aroma of God's love, will warm hearts in a special way.

A Moment to Ponder

How can you instill the sweet aroma of God's love in the hearts of children especially at Christmas?

A Memorable Christmas

The shepherds returned, glorifying and praising God
for all the things they had heard and seen,
which were just as they had been told.

LUKE 2:20 NIV

IMAGINE MARY GESTURING TO HER
NEWBORN BABY AS SHE TELLS THE
SHEPHERDS, "COME AND BEHOLD HIM—
JESUS, THE SAVIOR OF THE WORLD."

I love turning our house into a Christmas wonderland. The process begins with carrying the decorations from our storage room. It's fun unpacking those boxes. There are the Christmas carolers, the stockings that have hung on the mantel for years, and the village that brings a touch of ancient Bethlehem into our home.

Holiday dishes we've used at Christmas dinners for many years bring sweet memories of loved ones who once shared the holidays with us. There are nativity sets—one that's a treasure from my childhood, and another that we've used when the family reads the Christmas story together.

But there's one thing I always look forward to and that's unpacking our ornaments. Our family decorates the tree together. Now that our sons are grown and have families of their own, we plan an evening where everyone comes home to help us decorate the Christmas tree. Some ornaments are from my first Christmas. A few are from my dad's tree. It's like visiting dear old friends I haven't seen for a while.

The same is also true when I read the Christmas story during the holidays. I often read it throughout the year, but there's something special about reading it while we're celebrating the birth of God's Son. Imagine Mary and Joseph navigating the streets of Bethlehem. Picture a choir of angels serenading shepherds in the fields. Think about the holy hush in that rugged stable as those shepherds came to see if what the angels had told them was true. And smile as you imagine Mary gesturing to her newborn baby as she tells the men, "Come and behold him—Jesus, the Savior of the world."

God wants all of us to come close and behold his Son.

Father, thank you for the people in the Bible who have become like dear old friends as I've read their stories— people whose lives have become real to me. I can only imagine what it must have felt like for Mary to know that as she snuggled her newborn son, she was holding the salvation of the world in her arms. Thank you for that salvation and how it has touched my life.

A CHRISTMAS GIFT

Do you have friends who are senior citizens? Do you have friends or family members who are vision-impaired? The loss of sight can be difficult whether it's from disease or age. Make time during the holidays to visit those friends. Offer to read the Christmas story and some of their other favorite verses from the Bible to them. Or better yet, invite them to be part of your family events. You'll discover that you're the one who will receive the biggest blessing from this.

A Moment to Ponder

Imagine what it must have been like for Mary and Joseph on that first Christmas. What emotions do you think they felt?

I Love You More

Jesus replied: "Love the Lord your God with all your heart
and with all your soul and with all your mind."

MATTHEW 22:37 NIV

WHEN WE THINK OF THE LOVE WE HAVE FOR

JESUS, IT REMINDS US TO COME AND BEHOLD

HIM WITH OUR HEART, SOUL, AND MIND.

$\mathcal{M}$y friend and I met for lunch just before Christmas, and she told me about a cute God-moment she had with her youngest child. Their adopted son from China came to live in the United States at the age of six, weighing only thirty-seven pounds and in desperate need of heart surgery. Eight years old now, he is an active and healthy little boy. "And he loves video games," his mom said.

She shared about that day. "I was pushing him on the swing-set, and he said, 'Mommy, I love you more than a pine cone.' I laughed at his remark and returned his affection verbally.

"But, I couldn't help but think about what a difficult two years we'd had," she told me. "The language barrier, the separation anxiety, the health issues, sibling struggles, a more critical surgery than we expected. And I whispered this prayer when he ran in the house, 'God, I wish he loved me more than his video games.'

"Two days later, I was standing at the kitchen sink, and Noah was in the den, you guessed it, playing a video game. He yelled to me, 'Mommy, I love you more than a video game.' It felt like a Christmas gift from God to me."

As I was driving home from lunch with my friend, I couldn't help but smile at the boy's words and God's treat for my friend. It made me wonder if my actions show God that I love him more than a pinecone. Or my new van. Or my education. Or my upcoming vacation. Or my favorite piece of jewelry. Or any of my Christmas presents.

God sent his only Son to a lowly stable with instructions for me to love him more than anything on this earth. Nothing else can or should compare with my love for Jesus. Nothing should even come close to the love that I feel for my Savior. When I think of the love that I have for Jesus, it reminds me to come and behold him with my heart and my soul and my mind.

Lord, I love you more than anything this world has to offer. Forgive me when my actions don't show that to you. Help me love you with my heart and my soul and my mind as an all-inclusive, package deal.

A CHRISTMAS GIFT

Many, many children will spend the Christmas season longing for a forever home and forever family. Take time to pray for foster families, foster kids, and children in orphanages and group homes. If you know a foster family in your church or community, reach out to them to ask how you can help meet some of their needs over the holidays.

A Moment to Ponder

How did Mary and Joseph's actions—from the time Mary found out she was pregnant to the delivery of baby Jesus—reveal their love for God? How do your daily activities show that you love God with your heart and soul and mind?

The Most Special Gift

She gave birth to her first son. Because there were no rooms left in the inn, she wrapped the baby with pieces of cloth and laid him in a feeding trough.

LUKE 2:7 NCV

ALL WE HAVE TO DO IS COME AND

BEHOLD HIM—THE ONE WHO LOVES US

WITH AN EVERLASTING LOVE—

AND ACCEPT THE GIFT THAT IS AVAILABLE.

Some family members save their wrapping paper from one Christmas to use at the next one. After several Christmases, the paper becomes bedraggled and the pieces become smaller, so it's not unusual to discover packages wrapped with a patchwork of multiple papers.

I have a friend whose Christmas gifts are so beautifully wrapped that they're works of art. Mine? Not so much. With all our kids and grandchildren, we have a lot of presents to wrap, so our gifts usually appear without any fancy toppings. I consider it an accomplishment just to get mine all wrapped—but they're wrapped with love.

One of my best childhood Christmas memories has to do with gift wrap. My aunt had a large family, and she also bought presents for all the extended family, neighbors, and friends. The pile of gifts under her tree was truly impressive.

One Christmas, my aunt decided she could remember what she'd wrapped for each person, so she didn't use gift tags. It was hilarious on Christmas Eve when we all gathered around the tree. Everyone was opening the wrong presents while my aunt tried to remember who the recipient of that package should be. Let's just say there were gift tags on all the gifts the next year.

The absolute best gift arrived in a humble stable many years ago to a young couple named Mary and Joseph. I imagine that like most first-time parents they wanted everything to be perfect for their newborn son—especially since they knew how truly special he would be. I'm sure they didn't plan for Jesus to be born in a stable and then wrapped in swaddling clothes (strips of fabric they wrapped around the baby).

But on that night so long ago, life changed forever. We were given the most precious gift we'll ever receive: love wrapped in swaddling clothes, lying in a manger. All we have to do is come and behold him—the one who loves us with an everlasting love—and accept the gift that is available for all of us: Jesus.

Father, your love amazes me. I'm so grateful that it's available to everyone. Just as the shepherds did, help me to share the good news about that blessed first Christmas and how that humbly-wrapped gift can change lives forever.

A CHRISTMAS GIFT

Ask God to place five people on your heart who need to hear about the love of Jesus and how it's available for them. Wrap a simple gift to give to them and as you hand it to them, explain that God's love is a gift just like that—all they have to do is accept it.

A Moment to Ponder

Think about the gift of that baby wrapped in swaddling clothes and how God's love has changed your life.

A Helping of Wisdom

The Child continued to grow and become strong,
increasing in wisdom;
and the grace of God was upon Him.

LUKE 2:40 NASB

IT IS A PRIVILEGE TO COME AND BEHOLD HIM

WHEN WE SEEK HIS WISDOM.

One of my favorite parts of Christmas was working in the kitchen with my mom and two grandmas to bake goodies for friends and family. I was in awe of their wisdom to prepare (without recipes) luscious fruit cakes, divinity, ambrosia, and more.

So, I was excited when my husband brought home a bag of gooey Friendship Bread starter and a page-long recipe. I couldn't wait to make homemade bread for my friends' Christmas presents. The directions that required ten days of attention sounded simple: squish the bag, add additional ingredients, squish again. But all I had was a lumpy mess and unfriendly goo that oozed onto my countertop.

"What am I doing wrong?" I whispered. I knew it was a silly request to ask God for cooking wisdom, but I recalled James 1:5 that says if we lack wisdom we should ask God because he wants to give it generously—so I made my request known.

The next time I attempted the recipe, I remembered Grandma's instructions from one of those Christmas baking days long ago and added my liquids slowly, stirring with a wooden fork to incorporate a little flour at a time. It worked. No more lumps. And four days later, I had a delicious cinnamon sweet treat for my friends.

Both of my grandmothers are in heaven now, but I still treasure the things they taught me. Christmas baking memories along with other fond ones, make me appreciate their wisdom. I love to think about Mary teaching sweet baby Jesus, toddler Jesus, and little boy Jesus. I find it fascinating to think about him growing in wisdom from that first day in the manger onward. How his parents, and perhaps grandparents, must have delighted in teaching him.

I've treasured opportunities to teach my children, and now my grandchildren, but I hope the wisdom I impart most fervently is to grow in Jesus all the days of their lives. I hope they'll readily ask God for wisdom and delight in his answers. It's a privilege to come and behold him when I seek his wisdom.

Oh, Jesus, how I treasure your wisdom. Thank you, God, that I can ask you for wisdom and you delight in sharing generously. Your wisdom surpasses all. I praise you and love you.

A CHRISTMAS GIFT

Gather everyone in the kitchen to make a cinnamon roll Christmas tree. On waxed paper, unroll a tube of crescent rolls. Brush the rectangle top with melted butter. Sprinkle with cinnamon sugar. Roll the dough jelly-roll fashion, beginning at one long edge. Use a serrated knife to cut the roll into twelve slices. Arrange them (on a lightly-greased baking sheet) into a Christmas-tree shape like this: one slice on the top row, two slices next, three slices on the third row, four slices on the fourth row, and two slices centered on the bottom for the tree's stem. Leave a little space between slices for the dough to expand while baking. Bake at 350 degrees for twelve to fifteen minutes, until golden. When cool, drizzle a powdered-sugar-and-milk frosting over the top. While working in the kitchen, ask the kids where their wisdom comes from. Remind them that God is the original wisdom giver.

A Moment to Ponder

Think about the gifts, talents, and wisdom that God has given you. How can you share these with someone this Christmas?

One Flame

Encourage one another and build each other up,
just as in fact you are doing.
1 Thessalonians 5:11 niv

YOUR FLAME MIGHT BE THE ONE THAT WILL
LIGHT THE DARKNESS FOR SOMEONE WHO
NEEDS TO SEE JESUS, WHO NEEDS TO COME AND
BEHOLD HIM IN ALL HIS BEAUTIFUL GLORY.

One of my favorite things about Christmas is the candlelight Christmas service at our church. The members gather on the Sunday evening nearest Christmas Day, and as folks walk into the main auditorium, each person receives an unlit candle. First-time visitors sometimes look puzzled as they receive theirs, but it always makes me smile because I know they're in for a special treat.

Our pastor talks to the congregation about unity in Christ and how it might sometimes seem as if our efforts don't amount to much as we each work individually for God. But when we all come together and work in one accord, great things happen for God, we are encouraged, and we become an encouragement to others.

As the pastor continues to speak, the building is darkened, the blackness so dense that none of us can see anything or anyone. But then he strikes a match and lights the candle he's holding. I'm always amazed by how that one tiny candle shows up in the darkness in our huge auditorium.

The pastor then lights the associate pastor's candle and then the two of them share the flame from their candles to the rest of the church staff. Each of them then takes a section of the auditorium and lights one candle at the end of each row. Each person shares the flame from his or her candle to the person next to them.

When everyone's candle is lit, our pastor does something that moves me to tears each time. He says, "Now, everyone, hold your candle high." The beauty of that moment as everyone stands together is indescribable, but none of it would have happened if that one solitary candle hadn't shared the flame.

This Christmas would be the perfect time to share the flame of Jesus. To work together for the one who came as a tiny babe in Bethlehem. Your flame might be the one that will light the darkness for someone who needs to see Jesus, who needs to come and behold him in all his beautiful glory.

Father, thank you for the beauty and significance of the candlelight service each Christmas. I'm so grateful that the darkness of my life was brightened by the flame of your love. Remind me that my individual work for you can make a difference, but that true power is found when we come together for you.

A CHRISTMAS GIFT

Look for ways that you can brighten the darkness for someone this Christmas. The holiday season is difficult for those who've lost a loved one, people who are going through a health crisis, people with financial difficulties, and those who feel alone. Hugs, cards of encouragement, gift cards for meals, presents for children who wouldn't otherwise receive gifts, and even the gift of your time will touch hearts and provide encouragement.

A Moment to Ponder

How can you make a difference this Christmas by sharing the flame that God lit in your heart?

A Reminder

"Be still, and know that I am God;
I will be exalted among the nations,
I will be exalted in the earth."

PSALM 46:10 NIV

WE JUST NEED TO BE STILL LONG ENOUGH

TO COME AND BEHOLD HIS PRESENCE.

Meow." I watched Snowflake dart up the stairs, halting just out of reach. No coaxing brought the feline closer, which didn't really matter—I didn't like him any more than he liked me. In fact, I was pretty sure he had only two fans: God and my mom. The feral stray wandered up to my mom's doublewide trailer five years ago, mangy-looking with ribs protruding like slats on our old barn. He wouldn't let anyone but Mama pet him.

Mama was the reason I was here to feed Snowflake. With Christmas just days away, Mama remained hospitalized in critical condition following a procedure that went awry. I'd had no time to think about baking or presents or the birth of Jesus. I prayed, yet God and healing and Christmas seemed out of reach—just like this cat. I felt angry at God for not healing Mama, for abandoning me, just like I was angry at this blasted cat for keeping his distance.

"*Meow.*" I stole a glance at Snowflake. *Wait—he's not stopping at his bowl this time. Is he actually walking toward me?*

Be still, I thought. Cautiously, Snowflake approached and brushed against my leg. His back arched to meet my fingers as he allowed me to pet him, then he ambled to his bowl. I smiled and a tear trickled down my cheek. I thought about how God had taken care of this feline. I thought about how God took care of Mary, Joseph, and a little baby. If God could take care of an unlikable cat and a much-loved baby, couldn't he take care of my mom?

In fact, hadn't he been doing so all along, but I was too worried and busy to notice? I just needed to be still long enough to come and behold his presence. I asked God to forgive me right there on the porch. Maybe God and healing—and my feelings for Snowflake—weren't quite so out of reach after all. Suddenly, the warmth of Christmas seemed much closer too.

God, forgive me when I let things in life, like a serious illness or even things of lesser importance, take my focus off you. Especially during Christmas, my thoughts should be about the precious baby in the manger. Thank you for hanging on to me, Lord, when I don't seem very reachable and for loving me unconditionally even when I act very unlovable.

A CHRISTMAS GIFT

Consider making a Christmas donation to a local animal shelter or animal fostering organization to help care for some of God's creations. Call and ask what items are needed, like food or treats, leashes or collars, and deliver a Christmas care package to meet some of those needs. If you're not already doing so, start keeping a prayer journal of prayer requests and praises to remind you that God listens when you pray.

A Moment to Ponder

What takes your focus away from God during Christmas? What practical things can you do to make sure that Jesus remains the most important part of each day during the holidays?

This Is for You

What shall I return to the Lord
for all his goodness to me?

<small>PSALM 116:12 NIV</small>

THE ONE GIFT WE CAN GIVE GOD THAT'S
SURE TO PLEASE HIM IS TO COME AND
BEHOLD HIM WITH LOVE, AND WHISPER,
"JESUS, THIS YEAR I GIVE YOU ALL OF ME."

$\mathcal{M}$y young son bounced with excitement, "I'm making you something for Christmas, but it's a secret." I made crazy guesses as to what it could be, but my little craftsman refused to divulge his secret.

On the last day before Christmas break, he carefully carried a bag as he walked from the classroom. When we got home, I sat on the couch as directed. My son placed the bag on my lap. His little face was so precious, "I made it just for you, Mama. I hope you like it."

"It" turned out to be a collection of slightly ragged ornaments cut from construction paper. There was an angel, a bell, a candle, a candy cane, and a green one shaped like a Christmas tree. All of them had been decorated with glitter, and on the back in those crooked letters used by those just learning to write, he'd painstakingly written his name, the year, or my favorite, *I luv u, Mama*.

Our family Christmas tree has some expensive ornaments on it, and some valuable collectible ones, but there are none I treasure more than those that my little boy made for me with love. Those paper ornaments have hung on our family tree for almost thirty years now, and it makes me feel loved every time I see them.

Sometimes we think that we have to do something big for God to show our love for him, but even the little things we do for him each day touch his heart. Just as my precious little boy gave me those homemade ornaments that he'd made with love, God will find value in the gifts we give him—whether it's spending time with him or helping someone else as if we were doing it for him.

God already owns everything in the universe, but the one gift we can give him this Christmas that's sure to please him, is to come and behold him with love, and whisper, "Jesus, this year I give you all of me."

Lord, you've blessed me way more than I've deserved, and I'm so grateful. I want to give you something to express my love for you, but everything I have is already a gift from you. This Christmas I give you all of me—my heart, my life, and my love.

A CHRISTMAS GIFT

Christmas is a great time to reflect on your life spiritually.
Pray and ask God to show you ways that you can please
him. Make a list of twelve things you can do to show
your love for God, and then choose one for each month
of the year as your gift to him. But be prepared because
it's impossible to out-give God, and you'll end up being
blessed as you seek to bless him.

A Moment to Ponder

Why is God's heart touched when we bring him our offerings
of love? Why is Christmas the perfect time to do that?

COME
AND
BEHOLD
HIM...

the Mighty
God

Holding Heaven

To us a child is born, to us a son is given;
and the government shall be upon his shoulder,
and his name shall be called Wonderful Counselor,
Mighty God, Everlasting Father, Prince of Peace.

ISAIAH 9:6 ESV

EACH CHRISTMAS WE CAN COME AND

BEHOLD HIM THROUGH HIS STORY,

WITH GRATITUDE IN OUR HEARTS.

The first Christmas with our six-month-old son was exciting. He was entranced by the lights on the tree and the bright colors of the ornaments. We held him in our arms and planned ahead for the fun we'd have with him at Christmas in the years to come. We talked about how we'd read the Christmas story together as a family each Christmas Eve so our son would always remember the birth of Jesus.

We added two more sons, three daughters-in-law, and seven grandchildren to the mix over the years, and for more than forty years, we've spent our Christmas Eve reading the Christmas story and praying together before we open gifts. It's my absolute favorite time.

We've all heard the oh-so-amazing Christmas story, but can you imagine actually *being* there that night? Being some of the first people to see the Messiah. Kneeling beside the manger for a close look at the child who would change the world. Sharing the joy of that moment with Mary and Joseph. It boggles my mind to imagine how extraordinary that time must have been.

I suspect that stable was a busy place the night Jesus was born. In their excitement, I imagine the shepherds stayed awhile when they came, all of them in awe at being part of this fulfilled prophecy told in the book of Isaiah.

Mary and Joseph were probably thrilled to have them there to celebrate the birth of Jesus, but I know they must have been glad when everyone left and they were finally alone with their baby boy. Like most new parents, they probably counted his fingers and toes. Stroked their fingers through his soft hair. Gazed at his sweet features and cuddled him close.

Unlike most new parents, they knew that when they snuggled the babe in their arms, they were holding heaven, holding the one who would become the salvation of the world.

We didn't have the opportunity to be there that night so long ago, but each Christmas we can come and behold him through his story, with gratitude in our hearts.

Dear Jesus, the story of your birth never gets old. Because a babe came to a manger, I can hold a piece of heaven in my heart, and I can celebrate the salvation that you give so freely to everyone. And because of that, my life has been changed forever. Thank you for loving me that much.

A CHRISTMAS GIFT

Put together a family play and act out the Christmas story. Gather housecoats for the shepherds and Joseph and put together a simple outfit for Mary. A baby doll wrapped in strips of fabric can serve as the baby Jesus. And then take your show on the road, stopping at each of your neighbor's houses to perform the Christmas story for them. Print out Luke 2:1-16, roll the paper up, tie it with a pretty ribbon, and leave one at each house.

A Moment to Ponder

What do you think it was like to be there on the night that Jesus was born? How do you think you would have reacted?

Make Haste

When the angels went away from them into heaven, the shepherds said to one another, "Let us go over to Bethlehem and see this thing that has happened, which the Lord has made known to us." And they went with haste and found Mary and Joseph, and the baby lying in a manger.

LUKE 2:15-16 ESV

ANY TIME,
NOT JUST SPECIAL OCCASIONS,
CAN BE AN OPPORTUNITY TO
COME AND BEHOLD HIM.

*T*uck in your shirt and please tie your brother's shoes,"
I said over my shoulder as I hit the bottom stair. "Brush
your hair; please find your sister's other black shoe, and
take her potty," I said a little louder from the middle of the
stairs. "Do you mind putting the food away while I brush
my teeth, throw on some make-up, and find a shirt without
stains to wear?" I bellowed that request, because by now, I'd
made it to the top of the stairs.

It was Christmas Eve and I was scrambling to get our family
of six ready for church. I was excited: the services were
always extra-special this time of year.

Where in the world are my shoes? I pondered, as I rounded
the corner.

Crack. "Ow!" I yelled and hit the floor. I'd managed to snag
my right pinky toe on the tall, wooden chest of drawers.

Still searching for the shoes that needed tying, the five-
year-old came to my bedroom. "Mommy?"

"Go get your daddy, please."

I wouldn't be heading to church but to the ER, shoeless, to
repair the little toe that was now at a perfect right angle to
the four remaining toes.

My haste hadn't served me well earlier, but I wondered, as I stared at my foot on the gurney, do I always look forward to seeing Jesus with such anxiety? I expected the Christmas Eve service to be moving, with angelic children singing, the fourth graders reenacting that night long ago, and the pastor reminding us that a perfect baby would grow into the sinless man that would die for *my* sins.

Yes, church services at Christmas are extra special. But I'm sure God wants me to be that excited about seeking him always. I made a mental note that any time—not just special occasions—can be an opportunity to come and behold him.

I just hope the shepherds made haste that night more cautiously than I did.

Lord, help me seek you with the same haste that the shepherds of long ago did. May I be enthralled with that which you've made known to me, through Jesus, on a daily basis, not just on special occasions like Christmas, Easter, or Sunday mornings. Open my eyes every day to see the good tidings that you bring.

A CHRISTMAS GIFT

Do you know someone who might not be able to attend church services this year due to an injury, sickness, or other circumstance? Consider baking a special treat and make haste to visit that person, bringing good tidings and Christmas joy when you go.

A Moment to Ponder

What steps can you take to seek Jesus year-round with the same excitement that Christmastime brings?

Sharing Christmas

When they had seen Him, they made widely known the saying which was told them concerning this Child. And all those who heard it marveled at those things which were told them by the shepherds.

LUKE 2:17-18 NKJV

WE CAN SHARE
THE STORY OF JESUS—
TO INVITE OTHERS TO
COME AND BEHOLD HIM.

$\mathcal{A}$ country church in our town goes the extra mile at Christmas with their drive-through live Nativity. It's a true labor of love. Hundreds of church members volunteer their time and talents—building sets, making costumes, hauling farm animals in for the weekend, directing traffic, and becoming townsfolk for the city of Bethlehem.

It's one thing to read the Christmas story or to listen to someone reading it, but to see living, breathing people in those roles, to hear the sounds of the animals at the stable, and to experience a makeshift village of Bethlehem, makes it all so real.

The narrated tour starts by taking us by the inn—where there was no room for Joseph and Mary (and the impending birth of Jesus). In another scene, shepherds watch over their sheep in the field, and the next stop features a choir of angels singing as they celebrate the birth of Jesus. The white-robed angels are stunning as they're spotlighted against the darkness of the night.

The drive-through ends with the scene we're all familiar with from Christmas cards and manger scenes in our homes. But at this one, sheep wander around and cows moo. A donkey stands guard near the manger. Outside the stable, the aroma of smoke from the cooking fire fills the air. Mary's face is tender as she cuddles her newborn son, and Joseph looks on in awe. Shepherds bow in worship as they meet the King of kings.

A holy hush fills the air as the story takes on life. It always moves me to tears of gratitude for the most precious gift ever given.

What a beautiful gift for our community as the church members share the news about the arrival of that babe in the manger—and how his life will also change our lives forever. And what a great reminder for the rest of us to share the story of Jesus with our neighbors, co-workers, family, and friends—to invite others to come and behold him.

Lord, the story of Jesus is the best story ever told, yet I sometimes hold onto it like a well-kept secret. Remind me that there are others who haven't yet heard the story of your birth and the reason why you came. Help me to share that news with the excitement that it deserves.

A CHRISTMAS GIFT

Does your church support missionaries around the world? Are there children in need in their areas? Consider supporting a child every month. Ask if the missionaries could use toys, clothing, or other supplies. Send money for Christmas dinner for an orphanage—whether across the sea or here at home—or send Christmas decorations for the missionaries who are far from home and family. Be an encouragement in honor of Jesus.

A Moment to Ponder

Why is Christmas an especially good time to share our faith? What are some ways that you and your family can do that this Christmas?

A Lowly Setting

*While they were there,
the time came for the baby to be born.*

LUKE 2:6 NIV

COME AND BEHOLD A SAVIOR WHO MAKES
IT POSSIBLE FOR US TO HAVE A SWEET
RELATIONSHIP WITH OUR HEAVENLY FATHER.

$\mathcal{G}$ingerbread Lane, on display each year at the New York Hall of Science Museum in Queens from early November to mid-January, holds the Guinness World Record for the largest gingerbread village for the last several years. To qualify for the title, every part of the magnificent display must be edible. The exhibit has to exemplify a real village, with houses, shops, and public service locations.

The massive holiday display requires more than six hundred pounds of gingerbread, almost five thousand pounds of frosting, and eight hundred pounds of candy. Colored candies pressed into frosting become sidewalks. Red-and-white-striped candy canes line stairways. Red and green M&M's dot rooftops, and jelly beans transform into roofing shingles.

Regular visitors to Gingerbread Lane wait in anticipation for opening day of the delectable village. And, finally, the day arrives. The luscious village fills the air with the aroma of ginger, cloves, cinnamon, and sweetness. One might even gain a pound or two just gazing at the display.

The work of art created by chef Jon Lovitch takes practically an entire year to complete, from conception of ideas to hand-drawn sketches on a notepad, from baking and assembling, to frosting and embellishing, to transporting to the museum. The final product takes months to come to life.

Mary and Joseph waited nine months for Jesus' appearance. I wonder how Mary prepared for the birth of her first child. Did she draw sketches of how she thought he'd looked as a baby? Did she make lists of needs for his arrival? Did she gather cooking staples she might need after his birth? She certainly didn't bake bread ahead of time, because, after all, she was journeying to Bethlehem instead.

Jesus' arrival was the most spectacular display of God's planning, preparations, and delivery. No gingerbread village could ever compete with *that* final product, right? When I think about gingerbread houses and villages often seen this time of year, I'm reminded of the hymn from long ago, *'Tis So Sweet to Trust in* Jesus because nothing compares to my sweet Savior, even sugar-laden gingerbread houses.

God, thank you for sending my sweet Savior in the form of a little baby so many years ago. Help me remember this season that nothing compares to the sweet relationship I have with you because you sent a baby long ago to make that possible.

A CHRISTMAS GIFT

Purchase a package of gingerbread cookies or make a batch of homemade ones and use icing to write the names of those who were there on the night Jesus was born. Save out some cookies to share with a neighbor. Gather the kids or grandkids and read the Christmas story aloud. Then let the kids use some of the cookies to retell the story. Have the kids accompany you to deliver the neighbor's cookies and encourage them to share the story of the birth of Jesus in their own words to the neighbor.

A Moment to Ponder

While nibbling on a gingerbread cookie, think about how it's a sweet treat to have a relationship with our heavenly Father. Then see if you can recall the entire Christmas story from memory.

Treasures for the Heart

Mary treasured up all these things
and pondered them in her heart.

LUKE 2:19 NIV

IT'S EASY TO COME AND BEHOLD HIM

WHEN WE PAY ATTENTION

TO WHAT'S REALLY IMPORTANT.

$\mathcal{A}$ highlight of my Christmas for many years was the annual production of my daughter's Nutcracker ballet. I treasure the memories I have of my little toy soldier, my flower, and my Sugar Plum Fairy.

I volunteered as a backstage mom each year to help with fast costume changes. One year, I was particularly anxious while standing in the wings, because I was so far behind in my Christmas preparations. Visions of my lengthy to-do list danced through my head. I even remember whispering, "I'll be glad when Christmas is over this year."

The striking of Tchaikovsky's first notes brought me back to the dress rehearsal. My daughter was the lead maid for this scene, and she assisted the Stahlbaums with their celebration. Party children and party parents entered in bold, royal colors, pretend gifts in hand.

Suddenly, there was confusion on the stage. The dance instructor stopped the music. "What happened, parents? Why weren't you in place?"

My daughter, who adores her dance teacher, spoke up. "It's my fault, Mrs. Shay. I just wasn't paying attention, and I didn't get there in time." Her teacher chuckled, thanked her for her honesty, and cued the music again.

Was that my problem this year? Was I not paying attention to what was really important: the birth of the child who came to save the world for all eternity? Was I letting the parties to attend, gifts to wrap, and desserts to bake crowd my head so Jesus couldn't find room?

Mary certainly didn't do that. She had plenty to think about: the responsibility of raising God's Son, caring for a newborn baby, and the pronouncements by the angels and shepherds. Yet Mary paid attention to what was most important—the little baby she held close to her heart. She pondered how this perfect little one would save the sins of all mankind and bridge the gap between sinful man and a holy God. Like Mary, it's easy to come and behold him when I pay attention to what's really important.

Dear Jesus, please help me remember what's really important—not the gifts or decorations or baking. You, Jesus. You are the reason for the season. Please let me keep you front and center of my heart, always.

A CHRISTMAS GIFT

Do you know someone with a new baby? Offer to babysit for an afternoon so that mom and dad can have a much-needed date, a chance to go Christmas shopping, or free time to bake or wrap presents. Be sure to sing "Jesus Loves Me" when you're rocking the precious newborn to sleep.

A Moment to Ponder

Think back to the birth of your first child, niece, or nephew. What kinds of thoughts went through your head about taking care of the baby? How might those thoughts have been like the ones Mary pondered in her heart? How might they have been different?

COME

AND

BEHOLD

HIM...

the Everlasting Father

Leftover Christmas Cards

Be anxious for nothing, but in everything
by prayer and supplication with thanksgiving
let your requests be made known to God.

PHILIPPIANS 4:6 NASB

WHEN WE COME AND BEHOLD HIM IN
PRAYER, LIVES CHANGE, BURDENS LESSEN,
AND HEARTS ARE BONDED TOGETHER.

*M*ost of us love to get personal mail, and Christmas is especially fun because of the cards that arrive each day. We love to see who we've heard from, to enjoy the family pictures tucked in many of them, and to read the Christmas newsletters that share the happenings of their lives.

Christmas cards are always so beautiful, whether they feature cute photos of dogs in holiday finery, favorite family pictures, snowy farmhouse wonderlands, or paintings depicting the scene in Bethlehem the night Jesus was born.

I've kept special cards through the years, sweet crayon drawings or hand-lettered homemade cards from my sons, sweet ones from my husband, and ones from beloved family and friends. They've taken on extra significance as my boys are now daddies with their own families, and as precious loved ones are now with Jesus.

But several years ago, our family began a new tradition. After Christmas, we keep the cards we've received, and each week, we pull one out and pray for the family or person who sent the card to us. We send them a note to let them know we're praying for them and ask if they have any special requests. It's always neat to see how God's timing is perfect as they send their replies.

We set out to do this as a blessing for our family and friends, but it turned out to be a bigger blessing for us, one that has deepened our love for these folks who are already special to us.

Maybe your family would also like to use your Christmas cards to pray for your loved ones. Or perhaps you'd rather do it together through the holidays, praying for your family and friends as the cards arrive.

Whatever you choose, the gift of prayer never goes out of style, never grows old, and always fits. Honoring the birth of Jesus by praying for those he came to earth for seems so right, doesn't it? When we come and behold him in prayer, lives change, burdens lessen, and hearts are bonded together.

Father, I'm so grateful for the precious family and friends you've placed in my life. Remind me to share the gift of Christmas throughout the year as I have the privilege of praying for those that I love. Bless their lives as you have blessed me so abundantly.

A CHRISTMAS GIFT

Buy an extra box or two of Christmas cards, and then make a list of senior citizens, shut-ins, and nursing home residents. Send a few Christmas cards each month and explain that since the gift of Jesus is good throughout the year, you're sending love letters on his behalf. Let them know you're praying for them and that you love them. These people are often lonely, and you will make their day.

A Moment to Ponder

How has the gift of prayer touched your life at Christmas and through the year? How do you think your gift of praying for your family and friends will touch God's heart?

A New Adventure

*This is the day that the Lord has made;
let us rejoice and be glad in it.*

PSALM 118:24 ESV

THROUGH NEW EXPERIENCES,
GOD GIVES US OPPORTUNITIES TO COME AND
BEHOLD HIM IN JOYOUS ADVENTURE.

Growing up in the south, my husband and I had never experienced snow besides occasional light dustings. As you can imagine, the first significant snowfall we experienced mere days before Christmas brought out the inner kid in both of us.

We bundled up our 18-month-old son, four-year-old daughter, and seven-year-old son and made our way to a snow-covered hill. With great optimism, my mother-in-law had given us sleds before our move.

My husband lugged the Red Flyer wood and metal sled to the top of the hill. My oldest son pulled the aqua-colored, plastic, tub-like sled behind him. My daughter practically danced up the hill, and I carried the reluctant toddler in his red, puffy one-piece covering.

Dad and the two older children climbed aboard the wooden sled, and off they went. Little sister squealed with delight and threw her hands in the air, feeling safe with her daddy's arms wrapped around her.

The toddler and I rode in the plastic sled just seconds behind them, snowflakes stinging our faces and wind causing tears to trickle down our cheeks. Well, actually, the baby's tears were his own. The youngest child wasn't as adventurous as the older two, but he eventually warmed up to the fun.

Trudging up and sliding down the hill, I had the chance to admire God's beautiful creations. Fresh fallen snow. Tall evergreen trees. A small pond in the distance. The farmer's cattle huddled for warmth in a field. And families—moms, dads, and kids. I was fascinated by the beauty surrounding me, and I thanked God for his handiwork. It was a great day for rejoicing.

Through a new experience for our family, God gave us an opportunity to come and behold him in joyous adventure as we encountered the surprise of sledding downhill at top speed. And I marveled at the way God gives good gifts to his children at Christmastime—wrapped packages, holiday feasts, the fellowship of extended family, and a babe in a manger.

God, thank you for each new day and the adventure that it holds. Help me to remember that every day is just that—a gift from you to be enjoyed—and to rejoice in your goodness. Thank you, God, for fun family adventures during the holidays. May I treasure them always.

A CHRISTMAS GIFT

Gather the family in the kitchen to make edible sleds to share with someone special. You'll need two large peppermint candy canes, a graham cracker square, and a dab of frosting. Use a knife to spread a line of frosting on the bottom edges of opposing sides of the graham cracker square. Place the cracker on the candy canes so the frosting sits atop the straight parts of each candy cane, with the top part of the candy canes curving back over the cracker. The candy canes should resemble sled runners. Place wrapped chocolates on top of the cracker for Christmas packages. Write a note that says, "It's snow nice knowing you! I'm glad God put you in my life." Attach the note to the sled with red ribbon and share with a neighbor or friend.

A Moment to Ponder

What family adventures or vacations have you experienced at Christmastime? Do you remember to treasure those as gifts from God?

Serving Others

*Do not merely look out for your own personal interests,
but also for the interests of others.*

Philippians 2:4 nasb

WE CAN COME AND BEHOLD JESUS

WHEN WE ARE TAKING CARE

OF THOSE HE LOVES.

started a Christmas tradition when my kids were little to find a new way each year to serve someone in the community. One year, we canceled classes for the morning and baked sugar cookies. After all, we measured, counted, sorted, and even sampled. Surely that was satisfactory academia for my second grader, preschooler, and one-year-old.

Oh, and we practiced handwriting when we added notes that said, "Thank you, God, for baby Jesus," and "Happy Birthday, Jesus," and "God loves you."

We waited in the lobby of the homeless shelter while the director spoke to a couple inside her office. "I'm sorry that our shelter is full, but I can give you bus money to get to the next closest shelter," we overheard. A few minutes later, the back door closed.

The director thanked us for the cookies and smiled at the kids. Soon, we were on our way home.

At the end of the parking lot, I spied a young couple with a baby, waiting at the bus stop. The mom held the infant on her hip, and the dad lugged a large trash bag. My heart sank as I realized that this had to be the couple that was headed to the next shelter. I had a flashback of our recent move that year and remembered box after box of household goods that took weeks to unpack in our new apartment.

And this family fit everything they owned into one large garbage bag.

I thought about Mary and Joseph, with no place to lay their heads that night or perhaps later on in their escape to Egypt. I thought about Jesus' homelessness during his ministry. *God, the needs are great in this world. I need to do more than bake a plate of cookies at Christmastime. Help me to do my part.*

It dawned on me that I can come and behold Jesus when I am taking care of those he loves. And I couldn't wait to get home to make plans to do just that.

Jesus, thank you for loving me and all of humanity so much that you were willing to die on the cross for our salvation. Please remind me often that helping someone in need is one way to worship and serve you. Help me instill in my children and grandchildren a passion and love for helping others— at Christmastime and every other day of the year too.

A CHRISTMAS GIFT

As a family, brainstorm ideas for serving others in your community. Write each idea on a note card and place the cards in a basket. Set the basket somewhere that it can be seen regularly to remind you of your year-round gift for Jesus. Throughout the year, pull out a card and complete the project as a family. Add new cards to the basket as ideas of ways to serve Jesus by caring for those he loves pop into your head throughout the year.

A Moment to Ponder

Jesus took on human form and came to this world to die for all. How does that make you feel about helping someone in their time of need?

Seeking Jesus

After Jesus was born in Bethlehem of Judea in the days of Herod the king, behold, wise men from the east came to Jerusalem, saying, "Where is he who has been born king of the Jews? For we saw his star when it rose and have come to worship him."

Matthew 2:1-2 ESV

WHEN WE COME AND BEHOLD HIM IN THE LITTLE THINGS, WE DISCOVER THAT SEEKING JESUS LEADS TO A LIFETIME OF PRECIOUS BLESSINGS AND A SWEET RELATIONSHIP WITH HIM.

On the night that Jesus was born, the shepherds searched to find the baby that the angels had told them about. The wise men saw the star, and they looked for Jesus as well. They provide a wonderful lesson in how all of us should constantly seek after Jesus.

Familiar items at Christmas will provide glimpses of Jesus and sweet spiritual lessons if we'll just look for them, and they're great opportunities to teach our children.

Piles of gifts under the tree are proof of God's blessings, and they can prompt us to share the gift of Jesus with others. The bright lights of Christmas candles shining from our windows and throughout our homes can remind us that Jesus is the Light of the World, and he wants us to be a shining light for him.

Our Christmas trees are reminders of the journey of Jesus from the cradle to the cross: a gift that our minds can't even wrap around. Those ornaments that hang on our trees teach us that we can be living ornaments of God's love and grace.

Wish lists are always fun at Christmas, and it would be the perfect time for your family to make a wish list of ways that you can serve God in the upcoming year. Christmas carols give us a chance to celebrate Jesus in the same way that choir of angels did so long ago.

Nativity sets are wonderful prompts to share the amazing story of Jesus because some people have never heard it. A Christmas village reminds us to be a blessing to our neighbors and communities.

Our Christmas dinner provides an opportunity to think about hospitality and how we can share our family festivities with people who would otherwise be alone. And Christmas with a landscape of pristine snow reminds us to seek a pure soul that will please the heart of God.

When we come and behold him in the little things in our daily lives, we discover that seeking Jesus will lead to a lifetime of precious blessings and a sweet relationship with him.

Jesus, just as the shepherds and wise men did, help me to always seek after you. I want to know your heart. I want to please you. And I want to lead others to you. Thank you for the promise that all who seek you will find you.

A CHRISTMAS GIFT

Plan a family scavenger hunt to see how many spiritual lessons you can discover in your Christmas decorations and traditions. Post a Christmas Bible verse on your refrigerator and learn one for each week during Christmas. By the time your children are eighteen, they will have tucked seventy-two verses in their hearts. Teach your children to seek after the one who will never leave them or forsake them.

A Moment to Ponder

What are your favorite Christmas moments and traditions, and what can they teach you about Jesus?

The Christmas Journal

*Let this be written for a future generation,
that a people not yet created may praise the LORD.*

PSALM 102:18 NIV

GOD HAS GIVEN US THE PRIVILEGE TO COME
AND BEHOLD HIM WITH OTHERS, KNOWING
THAT CELEBRATING JESUS WILL BOND OUR
HEARTS TOGETHER FOR ETERNITY.

*M*any years ago, when my sons were still little, a dear friend gave me a Christmas book with pages where I could journal our Christmas memories. It's become one of my favorite possessions: a history book of our family's recollections from each Christmas.

Oh my, the treasures that have been tucked into the pages of that little book. There are "gift certificates" my sons put in my stocking that promised five-minute back rubs and other sweet things. There are hilarious lists of what they wanted for Christmas each year. It's fun to look at those lists now and realize that many of those toys are no longer made. And it's fascinating to see how their lists changed as they matured.

I kept a record each year of our guests for Christmas dinner, and now that some of those friends and family members have gone home to heaven, just seeing their names on the pages brings back such wonderful memories of times gathered around our table.

There are pages where I've shared my heart about what Christmas means to me, my thoughts about Mary and Joseph's journey to Bethlehem, and many other things about Christmas and Jesus that I want my family to someday be able to pass along to another generation. The gift of that babe in a manger is one that we can teach to our children, and they can teach to their children, and so on to future generations. A gift like that is too precious to keep to ourselves.

What better gift could I give my family than to know about a God who loves them so much that he came to earth to become their Savior? That he'll be their best friend. The one who will comfort them in difficult times. The God who has a purpose and a plan for their lives.

None of it would have happened if that babe in a manger hadn't come. And he's given us the privilege to come and behold him together, knowing that celebrating Jesus will bond our hearts together for eternity.

Lord, I thank you so much for the people who cared enough to tell me about a baby in Bethlehem and how he had touched their lives, and that he'd also touch mine if I'd let him. Help me to write the words that will lead my family to you, to share the story of a God who is so marvelous that there aren't enough words to describe him.

A CHRISTMAS GIFT

Purchase a Christmas journal for your family. Record your fun family memories and the history of what your family has done each Christmas. Best of all, write what's on your heart about Christmas, and about what Jesus means to you. Have each family member do the same, and by the time your children are grown, you'll have an awesome treasure.

A Moment to Ponder

Why is it so important for us to share the Christmas story with our families and with future generations? What are ways that you can do that?

COME
AND
BEHOLD
HIM...

the Prince
of Peace

Light in the Darkness

*The true light that gives light to everyone
was coming into the world.*

JOHN 1:9 NIV

WHEN THOSE TIMES OF DARKNESS ARRIVE IN
OUR LIVES, WE CAN COME AND BEHOLD HIM,
KNOWING THAT THERE'S NO BETTER PLACE
TO PUT OUR HEARTS.

---

*M*y young son sat on the stairs watching as I finished putting the lights on the tree. "A house just looks better with a Christmas tree in it," he said as he walked away. He's right. There's something about Christmas lights that makes everything look prettier.

A neighborhood in our town picks a weekend and passes out bags to all the neighbors. They place sand in the bottom and a candle, and then for the next three nights, they all light their luminaries so people can drive through and enjoy them. It's so lovely to look down every street and see the glow of those Christmas lights.

There's a house out in the country that takes Christmas lights to extremes. They probably have to start decorating in July (no exaggeration) to achieve the massive display that covers their acreage. My jaw dropped the first time I saw it, and the glow from the hundreds of thousands of lights is visible for miles before making it to their home.

Is it any wonder that Jesus—the Light of the World—made such a big impact on the night of his birth, and in the years that followed it? Many of us face darkness in our lives at Christmas: the loss of a loved one, the call from a doctor, a prodigal child, being alone, or dealing with job loss. It's difficult to feel joy at Christmas when our hearts are broken.

But that's where the light of Jesus brightens the darkness. Where hope unfurls. Where comfort arrives. Where provision is given. And where relationships are restored. All because of that babe in a manger who arrived all those years ago.

When those times of darkness arrive in our lives, we can come and behold the one who loves us so much that he gave his life for us, knowing that there's no better place to put our heartaches this Christmas than to place them into the hands of the one who sends light into the darkness.

Father, Christmas can be a difficult time when there is darkness in my life. I'm so grateful for the light you bring into those dark places, and for the unexplainable joy and peace you give me despite my circumstances. Help me to always celebrate your birth with the wonder that it deserves.

A CHRISTMAS GIFT

Do you have senior citizen friends or friends with health issues? Sometimes just simple things like carrying in the Christmas decorations can be difficult for them. Give your friends or neighbors a call and see how you can help them. Invite them to Christmas dinner at your house, and if they're not able to come there, send them a plate filled with your delicious meal. Or offer to do their Christmas shopping or wrapping for them. It's a great way to get your children involved and to teach them compassion at the same time.

A Moment to Ponder

Christmas is a great time to think about the things we often take for granted, like family, friends, health, and the light he brings into our lives. All of these are gifts from God. Let's give him the gift of grateful hearts this Christmas.

The First Christmas Baby

"This is eternal life, that they may know you,
the only true God, and Jesus Christ whom you have sent."

JOHN 17:3 NRSV

THINK ABOUT BABY JESUS TAKING HIS

FIRST BREATH AND BE REMINDED

THAT YOU CAN COME AND BEHOLD HIM

AS THE GIVER OF ETERNAL LIFE.

---

*A*n acquaintance of mine is a labor and delivery nurse on the night-time shift at the hospital in my hometown. I ran into her at a coffee shop when we were both taking a break from Christmas shopping. She had a rare night off, and I needed a hot chocolate to give me the energy to mark more items off my list.

Our tables were close together, and we chatted while our hot drinks cooled slightly. I asked her if she ever got tired of working at night, especially during the holidays. She quickly shook her head. "I have the unique profession that allows me to witness the miracle of life every day," the 18-year-veteran explained.

She harbored no bitterness about working on holidays at all. "It's just part of being a nurse," she said. She beamed when she added, "That pure joy when they hear the baby cry for the first time, makes every long shift worth it. Not everybody can say they've been with people on the best day of their lives."

She said that she and her colleagues especially love Christmas babies. "We wait anxiously," she said, "for that December 25th baby. It's a celebration."

The only baby I delivered close to a holiday was my July darling, and I was home by the time the fireworks exploded. It felt fitting to hear the booming sound of merriment as I rocked my precious miracle of life to sleep that night.

I wonder how Mary and Joseph celebrated their Christmas baby. They'd just witnessed the miracle of life. But, more importantly, the new parents were holding in their arms the miracle of eternal life, the one who would grow up to be the Savior of the world and give everlasting life to all that would come to him.

When I think about baby Jesus taking his first breath of life, I'm reminded that I can come and behold him as the giver of eternal life—to me and to all who come to him.

God, thank you for sending your Son on that first Christmas, delivered with little fanfare in the moment, but what a celebration it would turn out to be for all mankind. Thank you for the promise of eternal life through those first newborn cries that echoed into the night.

A CHRISTMAS GIFT

Many people don't have the luxury of celebrating Christmas with their family and friends because of their professions. Law enforcement officers and other public servants as well as many medical personnel spend that time away from loved ones. Hopefully, they get to celebrate at other times. Remember to pray for those individuals and consider dropping off goodies or thank you notes to a nearby hospital or fire station for their celebration away from home.

A Moment to Ponder

How did the birth of Jesus change your life for eternity? What visible differences do others see because of your relationship with Jesus? Think of ways to celebrate his birth in the days and weeks ahead, beyond the typical holiday festivities.

Fear
Not

The angel reassured her, saying, "Do not yield to your fear,
Mary, for the Lord has found delight in you
and has chosen to surprise you with a wonderful gift."

LUKE 1:30 TPT

CHALLENGING TIMES GIVE US AN
OPPORTUNITY TO COME AND BEHOLD HIM
AS HIS FAITHFULNESS AND PROMISES
UNFOLD BEFORE US.

I'd been looking forward to my firstborn's second Christmas for months. Of course, I had enjoyed his first Christmas, but at seven-months-old, he slept for much of the festivities that year. I couldn't wait for him to open the chubby train toys to push atop the yellow, snap-together oval track. I knew he'd love the squeaking pull toy that was stuffed in the closet. And, oh my, wouldn't he just adore the spiral ramp that allowed purple, blue, and yellow balls to roll and spin and tumble to the floor over and over again each time he chased and replaced the balls?

Yes, Christmas with an 18-month-old promised a grand time. That is, until my husband received orders late November for his first deployment. And he was leaving in just a couple of weeks. A military wife of five years, I knew this day might come. I held it together when we first got the news, planning logistically how to handle an unknown amount of time as a single mom, and what to do if the unthinkable happened during the war.

But one night, emotion and exhaustion gave way to tears— lots of them. My husband held me close and wiped the moisture from my face. "Try not to worry, darling," he said. "God's got this. He'll take care of you and our son."

Fear not. Such powerful words. When I'm confronted with fear and doubt, I think back to God's presence during that deployment. I remind myself that challenging times give me an opportunity to come and behold him as his faithfulness and promises unfold before me.

I can't imagine the thoughts and fear that must have coursed through Mary's veins at the sight of Gabriel and the implications of his words. She too was facing the unknown. In fact, according to law, Mary could have faced death. I'm sure she worried about what people would say about her situation. Yet Mary put her faith in God and believed Gabriel when he told her that God would be with her. And he was—for every day of her life.

Thank you, God, that you were with Mary when she was frightened. Thank you, Father, that you promise to be with me always. Help me to especially feel your presence when something causes me to be fearful. I trust you to be my shield and my protector, and for that I am so thankful.

A CHRISTMAS GIFT

Choose an afternoon or evening to write notes to soldiers. Gather family members, colorful stationary, writing utensils and markers, and write friendly sentiments to deployed men and women. Several websites online offer addresses and suggestions for sending personal messages to those who might be far from home and family over the Christmas holidays.

A Moment to Ponder

Think of a time when you experienced fear. How did God reveal himself to you during that frightening experience?

The Imperfect Tree

God made him who had no sin to be sin for us, so that in him we might become the righteousness of God.

2 Corinthians 5:21 NIV

To know that we are made perfect
by the blood of the one who spent
his first night in a manger
invites us to come and
behold him with thanksgiving.

When I was a little girl, I dreamed of the perfect Christmas tree. The ones like my friends had: symmetrical blue spruce varieties or manicured Frasier firs with exquisite glass ornaments that glittered like gold. Or an artificial one with pristine branches and tinsel that sparkled, though I'll admit I loved the aroma of our family trees.

We couldn't afford any of those with my father's meager farming salary. Every year, we cut a tree from the woods behind our old dilapidated farmhouse. A prickly eastern red cedar with lance-like leaves that smelled delightful but shed needles faster than you could curl ribbon. Never perfectly-shaped, the branches were twisted and gnarled. Bare spots highlighted flaws underneath. And gaping holes were unforgiving on the evergreens.

Once adorned with bulbs larger than my hand and decorated with cheap dime-store decorations and enough silver icicles to fill in nature's creativity, however, the tree sufficed and smelled of earth and Christmas and home.

When I met my city-boy husband-to-be who loved the outdoors, he said, "It's a wonderful life when you can cut your own tree." That city-boy was frugal, too. I'll admit, the idea grew on me more with each additional child, because they delighted in cutting a tree on Papa's and Mema's land. Our youngest son held the tree while Dad sawed. Our daughter liked to shimmy up a tree in the woods to confiscate mistletoe. The oldest helped his daddy carry the tree to the truck as our daughter danced and twirled amongst the shrubs.

The first time we lived too far away, I wept when I realized I'd finally have that perfectly-coiffed tree. I'd come to treasure those misshapen Christmas evergreens because it reminded me that God loves imperfect me. Despite my flaws, sins, mistakes, bare spots, and gaping holes, my perfect Father loves me with an everlasting love.

To know that I am made perfect by the blood of the one that spent his first night in a manger invites me to come and behold him with gratefulness and thanksgiving.

Dear God, thank you for sending your Son for imperfect me. Forgive me for my sins that nailed Jesus to the tree so long ago. I am grateful that Jesus' blood covers my flaws and imperfections and allows me to have a relationship with you.

A CHRISTMAS GIFT

Take time to sit in front of your decorated tree to pray as a family. Thank God for his perfect Son, Jesus. Then head to a craft table to make a Christmas tree-shaped reminder of God's blessings. Let each person trace and cut out hand-shapes from green construction paper. (Make one yellow handprint shape and one brown one, too.) Write something you're thankful for on each handprint. Glue the green hand prints onto a poster board in a pyramid shape, like a tree, with the fingers pointing down. Glue just the wrist-part of the hand to give the tree a three-dimensional appearance. Glue the yellow handprint at the top of the tree, fingers pointing up, for the star. Glue the brown handprint centered on the bottom for the stem.

A Moment to Ponder

How does it make you feel to know that Jesus came to earth to die for your sins? What changes can you make in your daily life to reflect a grateful heart?

After

Christmas

It is good for me to draw near to God;
I have put my trust in the Lord God,
That I may declare all Your works.

PSALM 73:28 NKJV

WE CAN COME AND BEHOLD HIM

ANY TIME WE WANT.

I love the process of getting ready for Christmas, decorating the house and turning it into a warm, cozy, festive environment, inviting friends for holiday meals and get-togethers, and enjoying extra time making precious memories with family. It's a joy to send and receive Christmas cards (many of them to or from family and friends I haven't seen in a while) and to attend heart-warming Christmas plays and special programs at church.

The excitement of our grandchildren makes the holidays even more special, and it warms my heart to see their joy as we bake cookies together, and as they sample them. I love watching their sweet faces as we read the Christmas story, and then as they open their presents. These are precious and irreplaceable moments, and I'm grateful for all of them.

The whole season is a time of celebration, a birthday party for Jesus, a reminder of a God who loved us enough to leave heaven for us.

But there's one part of Christmas that I dread, and that's what happens *after* Christmas. It's not nearly as much fun to take the decorations down as it is to put them up. And then comes the worst part of all: the time to individually wrap all the breakable things, box everything up, and haul the boxes into the storage closet again. The festive aspect of the house is gone and everything looks drab and bare because our Christmas celebration is now officially over.

The same doesn't have to be true in our lives. With a little planning, *after* Christmas can be just as special as before. The good news is that the gift of Jesus doesn't end on Christmas Day, it begins there, and it's good all year. That gives us 365 days a year to tell others about our amazing God—about his mercy, grace, and love. That means that we can come and behold him any time we want. How could it get any better than that?

Father, thank you for Jesus—the gift that keeps on giving. Each day with him is a blessing beyond words. Help me to celebrate you, my amazing God, just as much after Christmas as I do during the holiday season, and to tell others about you, my faithful and loving Lord.

A CHRISTMAS GIFT

Another fresh year begins just a few days after Christmas. Ask Jesus to show you ways that you can serve him during the new year and for opportunities to tell others about him. This would be a great time to start an "I love you" jar. Keep scraps of paper and a pen next to the jar, and each day, write a short "I love you, God, because…" note to him. Pull those notes out at the end of the year and thank him for being a God who is worthy of your praise.

A Moment to Ponder

How can you celebrate Jesus throughout the whole year instead of just at Christmas?

COME
AND
BEHOLD
HIM...

Jesus

The Christmas Story

LUKE 2:1-19 NIV

In those days Caesar Augustus issued a decree that a census should be taken of the entire Roman world. (This was the first census that took place while Quirinius was governor of Syria.) And everyone went to their own town to register.

So Joseph also went up from the town of Nazareth in Galilee to Judea, to Bethlehem the town of David, because he belonged to the house and line of David. He went there to register with Mary, who was pledged to be married to him and was expecting a child.

While they were there, the time came for the baby to be born, and she gave birth to her firstborn, a son. She wrapped him in cloths and placed him in a manger, because there was no guest room available for them.

And there were shepherds living out in the fields nearby, keeping watch over their flocks at night. An angel of the Lord appeared to them, and the glory of the Lord shone around them, and they were terrified. But the angel said to them, "Do not be afraid. I bring you good news that will cause great joy for all the people. Today in the town of David a Savior has been born to you; he is the Messiah, the Lord. This will be a sign to you: You will find a baby wrapped in cloths and lying in a manger."

Suddenly a great company of the heavenly host appeared with the angel, praising God and saying,

"Glory to God in the highest heaven, and on earth peace to those on whom his favor rests."

When the angels had left them and gone into heaven, the shepherds said to one another, "Let's go to Bethlehem and see this thing that has happened, which the Lord has told us about."

So they hurried off and found Mary and Joseph, and the baby, who was lying in the manger. When they had seen him, they spread the word concerning what had been told them about this child, and all who heard it were amazed at what the shepherds said to them.

But Mary treasured up all these things and pondered them in her heart.

Christmas Traditions

MAKE A LIST OF CURRENT TRADITIONS YOU WANT TO KEEP,
AND OTHERS YOU'D LIKE TO START WITH YOUR FAMILY

Christmas Gifts

MAKE A LIST OF THE GIFTS YOU WOULD LOVE
TO BE ABLE TO GIVE THIS YEAR

_____

_____

_____

_____

_____

_____

_____

_____

_____

_____

_____

_____

_____

_____

_____

_____

_____

Christmas Blessings

MAKE A LIST OF HOW YOU CAN BLESS OTHERS
DURING THIS CHRISTMAS SEASON

_____

_____

_____

_____

_____

_____

_____

_____

_____

_____

_____

_____

_____

_____